Old MacDonald's Funny Farm

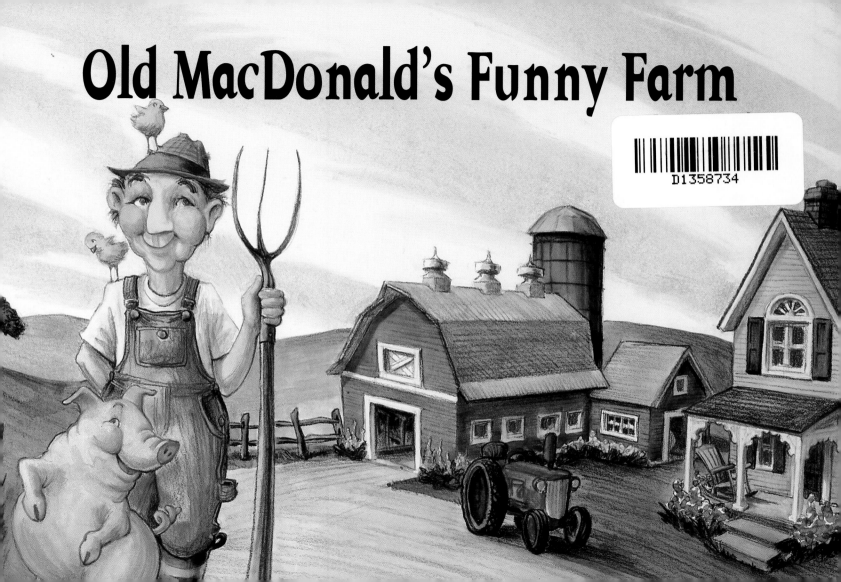

Old MacDonald had a farm.
Ee-i-ee-i-oh
And on the farm he had a shark.
Ee-i-ee-i . . . oh no!

Did you say a shark?
That's impossible!

Sharks live in the ocean.

Sharks are meat-eaters.

They have several rows of sharp teeth.

Sharks get air from the water through their gills.

Watch out for sharks!

4

Old MacDonald had a farm.
Ee-i-ee-i-oh
And on the farm he had a penguin.
Ee-i-ee-i . . . oh no!

Did you say a penguin?
That's impossible!

6

Some penguins live on the ice in Antarctica.
Penguins are funny-looking birds
that stand on short legs.
They waddle when they walk.
Penguins cannot fly,
but they are great swimmers.

Old MacDonald had a farm.
Ee-i-ee-i-oh

And on the farm he had a sloth.
Ee-i-ee-i . . . oh no!

Did you say a sloth?

That's impossible!

9

Sloths live in the rain forest.
Sloths hang upside down from tree branches.
They hardly ever go to the ground.
Sloths move so slowly
that they do not need to eat much food.

Old MacDonald had a farm.
Ee-i-ee-i-oh

And on the farm he had a tarantula.
Ee-i-ee-i . . . oh no!

Did you say a tarantula?

That's impossible!

Some tarantulas live in the desert.
This spider looks hairy and scary,
but its poison does not hurt people.
Tarantulas hunt insects at night.

Old MacDonald had a farm.
Ee-i-ee-i-oh

And on the farm he had a moose.
Ee-i-ee-i . . . oh no!

Did you say a moose?

That's impossible!

Moose live in forests.
Moose are the largest deer in the world.
They live alone, not in herds.
Moose like to eat water plants.

Old MacDonald had a farm.
Ee-i-ee-i-oh!

And on the farm he had a pig . . .

and a cow
and a horse
and a chicken
and a duck
and a turkey
and . . .

15

an elephant!

Ee-i-ee-i . . . oh no!